Searchlight
BOOKS™

Fake New

T0015774

What Is Propaganda?

Matt Doeden

Lerner Publications ◆ Minneapolis

Lerner Publications Company
An imprint of Lerner Publishing Group, Inc.
241 First Avenue North
Minneapolis, MN 55401 USA

For reading levels and more information, look up this title at www.lernerbooks.com.

Main body text set in Adrianna Regular.
Typeface provided by Chank.

Library of Congress Cataloging-in-Publication Data

Names: Doeden, Matt, author.
Title: What is propaganda? / Matt Doeden.
Description: Minneapolis : Lerner Publications, [2020] | Series: Searchlight books.
   Fake news | Audience: Ages 8–11. | Audience: Grades 4–6. | Includes bibliographical
   references and index.
Identifiers: LCCN 2018057824 (print) | LCCN 2019007428 (ebook) |
   ISBN 9781541556669 (eb pdf) | ISBN 9781541555761 (lib. bdg. :alk. paper) |
   ISBN 9781541574755 (pbk. :alk. paper)
Subjects: LCSH: Propaganda—Juvenile literature. | Fake news—Juvenile literature.
Classification: LCC P301.5.P73 (ebook) | LCC P301.5.P73 D64 2020 (print) |
   DDC 303.3/75--dc23

LC record available at https://lccn.loc.gov/2018057824

Manufactured in the United States of America
1-46031-43354-4/3/2019

Contents

 PAGE PLUS Scan QR codes throughout for more content!

Chapter 1

WHAT IS PROPAGANDA?

Since the late 1940s, a Communist government had controlled Poland. In 1989, an opposing party hoped to change that. The party's weapon was propaganda, and it came in the form of a poster.

The Solidarity social movement in Poland brought millions of citizens together in a nonviolent protest against Communism.

On June 4, 1989, the people of Poland voted to change from a Communist government to a democratic one.

The poster showed the sheriff from the American Western film *High Noon*. In his hand, the film's hero held a ballot with the Polish word for election. The message was clear. The opposition party was heroically standing up against Communism. Thousands of posters were put up around Poland. And they worked. Voters kicked out the Communist government. It marked a major change in Poland—and Eastern Europe. Some called it the poster that changed history.

Propaganda Basics

Propaganda is information crafted to form or change opinions about a topic. It often appeals to people's emotions. It stirs up feelings, such as patriotism, fear, or anger, to urge people to believe in an idea.

Propaganda is different from news because its creators are not trying to be objective. Propaganda does not present all sides of an argument. Some forms of propaganda are lies. Others present facts in ways that could be misleading or confusing.

This propaganda poster from World War II uses cartoon characters to represent the Germans defeating the British.

However, not all propaganda is untrue. For example, during World War I (1914–1918) and World War II (1939–1945), posters urged Americans to grow victory gardens. The message was that if people grew their own food, more could be sent to the troops overseas.

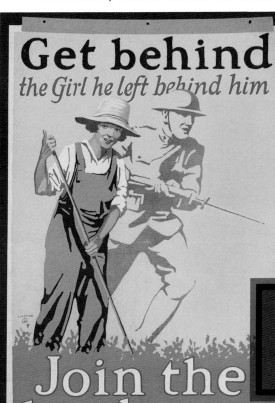

The information in the posters was true because facts are true by nature. But it was propaganda because it stirred up feelings of patriotism to get people to take action.

During World War I and World War II, Americans were encouraged to grow victory gardens.

Is Propaganda Harmful?

Many people think propaganda is bad, and often it is. During World War II, some propaganda showed Japanese Americans as dangerous and preparing to attack the United States. It was designed to scare other US citizens. It also built support for putting Japanese Americans in camps and preventing them from leaving until after the war ended.

WESTERN DEFENSE COMMAND AND FOURTH ARMY
WARTIME CIVIL CONTROL ADMINISTRATION
Presidio of San Francisco, California
May 3, 1942

INSTRUCTIONS
TO ALL PERSONS OF
JAPANESE
ANCESTRY
Living in the Following Area:

During World War II, posters like these instructed Japanese Americans to report to isolated communities called internment camps against their will.

POLITICAL ADS LIKE THE ONE SHOWN HERE
PLAY ON PEOPLE'S FEARS TO GET THEM TO
VOTE FOR AN OPPOSING CANDIDATE.

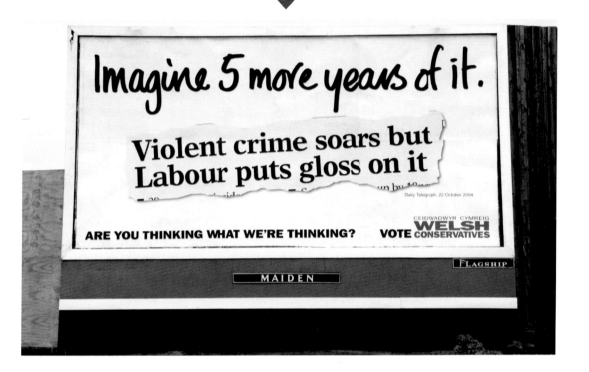

Other cases are less clear. Political ads use propaganda
to affect how people think. Voters may be warned that a
candidate doesn't care about children or will let criminals
out of jail. These ads may use quotes out of context, or
they may provide incomplete data. Their aim is to stir up
emotions to affect how people vote.

Real or Fake?

Is this story real or fake? See the Fake News Toolkit on page 29 to help you decide.

Vote Republican and Beat Terrorism

Terrorists want US voters to elect Hillary Clinton. Leaders of the terrorist group ISIS recently supported Clinton in the 2016 presidential election. ISIS leaders even threatened anyone voting for Trump.

Don't let the terrorists win!

Like   Comment   Share

Fake! Social media sites were full of stories like this during the 2016 election. It's made-up. An internet search would reveal that no trustworthy media sources reported it. The story provides no sources and clearly appeals to fear.

Scan the QR code to try another example.

Chapter 2

PROPAGANDA IN HISTORY

The history of propaganda dates back centuries, but it really took off when the printing press was invented in the fifteenth century. Suddenly, propaganda could be produced in large quantities.

After Johannes Gutenberg invented the printing press in the fifteenth century, books and other paper materials could be printed quickly and easily.

Propaganda and War

Nations soon learned the value of propaganda in wartime. During the American Civil War (1861–1865), the Northern (Union) states fought the Southern (Confederate) states. Northern propaganda painted Southerners as cruel slave owners.

This propaganda poster from the Civil War stirs up patriotism for the Union and refers to the Confederate states as traitors.

THE NORTH AND THE SOUTH WERE ENEMIES DURING THE AMERICAN CIVIL WAR, BUT THEY BOTH USED PROPAGANDA TO STIR UP EMOTIONS.

▼

Southern propaganda stirred up feelings of pride for the Confederate army. The North was painted as a threat to the South's way of life.

Propaganda was never more widely used than during World War II. Nazi Germany used everything from film to music to promote its message. German newspapers ran cartoons that presented white Germans as a "master race."

Adolf Hitler believed in a master race of Germans. He described his plans for Germany in his book *Mein Kampf*.

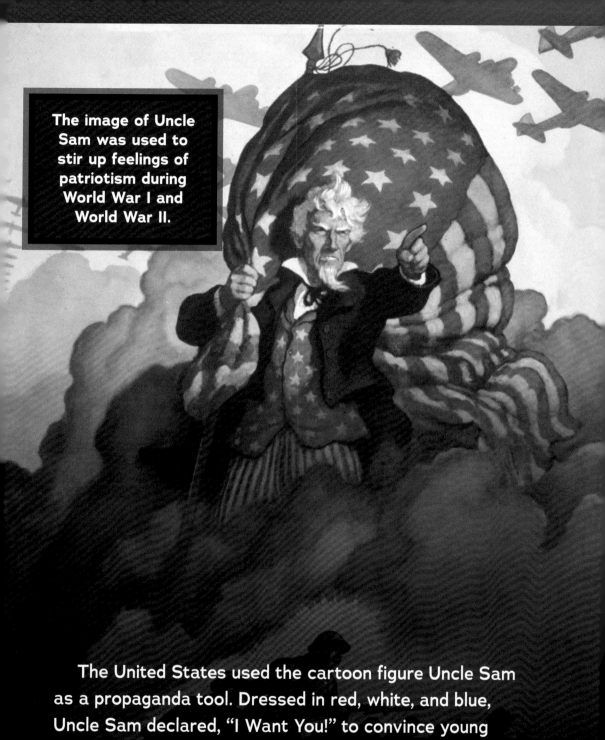

The image of Uncle Sam was used to stir up feelings of patriotism during World War I and World War II.

The United States used the cartoon figure Uncle Sam as a propaganda tool. Dressed in red, white, and blue, Uncle Sam declared, "I Want You!" to convince young men to join the military.

This is your brain.

this is drugs.

this is your brain on drugs.

Partnership For A Drug-Free America   N.Y., NY 10017

Client: Partnership for a Drug-Free America
Job # :   4D-235-AD
Size :   7" x 10"
Code :   DFPM-2127
Media :   TBD

Prepared by keye/donna/pearlstein

Social Propaganda

Propaganda isn't just about war. It plays a role in all areas of culture. For example, in a famous antidrug campaign of the 1980s, a television public service announcement (PSA) showed an egg. "This is your brain," explained the narrator. An image of a frying pan followed with the narrator saying, "This is drugs." Then he cracked the egg into the hot frying pan. As it sizzled, he added, "This is your brain on drugs. Any questions?"

Propaganda comes in many forms, including TV commercials.

Chapter 3

PROPAGANDA AND SOCIAL MEDIA

In this century, the rise of social media websites, such as Facebook and Twitter, allowed people to connect in new ways. Such sites quickly became the preferred type of media for sharing propaganda.

Social media differs from the mainstream media in several ways. Newspapers and network TV stations are expected to present news objectively. They are expected to give the full story, including all sides of an issue.

Unless they are presenting an opinion piece, TV and newspaper reporters state the facts of a story without giving their opinions.

News agencies try to give only objective information in online stories, whereas social media stories may appeal to emotion.

On social media, many groups present news in ways that support only one way of thinking. For example, a group that opposes immigration may post items that present immigrants as dangerous. A group that supports immigration might show pictures of hungry children needing help. Both posts try to use emotion to affect how readers view a subject.

Fake News

The idea of fake news grew with the rise of social media. A 2017 study showed that 67 percent of American adults get at least some of their news from social media. People often share false news stories without considering whether or not they're actually true. Often, they're not. Some are entirely made-up. Others are misleading.

With so many people reading news stories on social media, it's important to know what is real and what is fake.

In 2017, a video showing two boys in a fight went viral. The post claimed that a teenaged Muslim immigrant was attacking a boy on crutches. Many people shared the video to support the claim that immigrants and Muslims are dangerous. But police later learned that the attacker was neither Muslim nor an immigrant. That didn't stop people from sharing the video, and many who viewed it never knew the real story.

Jayda Fransen of a nationalist group called Britain First tweeted out a series of inaccurate videos casting Muslims in a negative light.

TWEETS
4

FOLLOWING
16

Tweets

Tweets

Jayda Fransen
@JaydaBF
Deputy leader of Britain First

London

Jayda Fransel
This is my off
website: brita

Franser

During the 2016 presidential election, one-sided stories divided Americans who had strong opinions about the candidates.

Social media propaganda is a powerful tool. In 2016, Russian groups set out to disrupt the US presidential election by flooding social media with propaganda. Strongly biased "news" articles were written to drive Americans apart. This made many people aware of the amount of fake news online. It also caused Facebook and other social media sites to change what they allow to be presented as news content.

Real or Fake?

Is this story real or fake? See the Fake News Toolkit on page 29 to help you decide.

DAILY NEWS

No. 49,725   THE BEST SELLING NEWSPAPER IN THE WORLD   Today's Edition

National - World - Business - Lifestyle - Travel - Technology - Sport - Weather

Eat Less, Live Longer

Hunger is good for your health. A study published in the journal *Nature Communications* shows that eating less helps mice—and people—live longer. Hunger changes the way cells function. They don't age as quickly, and they last longer. So, if you want to live longer, eat less!

View from the top

Lorem ipsum dolor sit amet, Consectetur adipiscing elit. Vivamus sit amet odio id lorem blandit luctus. Vivamus placerat viverra lorem. Vestibulum consectetur nunc vel sem laoreet dignissim. Cum sociis natoque penatibus et magnis dis parturient montes.

Consectetur adipiscing elit. Vi-

The best way to get something done is to begin

Donec sed turpis ligula. Vestibulum vitae dignissim eros, quis scelerisque lectus. Donec blandit

"Morbi lobortis lacinia, elit in suspendisse egestis, ullamcorper ligula erat,

Economy

Vivamus est elit, tristique id sollicitudin id, mattis et dolor. Morbi lobortis lacinia elit in euismod.

Real! It's true. Reducing calories in a responsible and healthy way does change how your body ages. Studies have shown this in mice, and research shows that it works for people too. How can you tell this story is real? The article gives a source for its information, a scientific journal. That's a good clue that you can trust what you're reading.

Scan the QR code to try another example.

Chapter 4

SPOTTING PROPAGANDA

We live in an information age. From TV to newspapers to the internet, news is everywhere. But not all news is created equally. It is up to each of us to understand what is real and what is not. Everyone should be a skeptic. That doesn't mean we should disbelieve everything. It does mean that we shouldn't accept everything we read, see, or hear as fact.

It can be hard to figure out what is a true story and what is fake news or propaganda. Just remember that not everything you see on the internet is true.

Suppose you see a story on social media about a political candidate. The story tells how the candidate wants to ban the use of plastics in all consumer products. It lists examples of how the laws the candidate supports will take away people's freedom to buy and use all items made of plastic. It may be convincing. It may make you feel surprised or even angry. But is it true?

As we learn more about how plastic bags are bad for the environment, many people feel they should be banned—but most people aren't calling for a ban on all plastic.

WHILE DISCUSSIONS OF BANNING
PLASTIC BAGS ARE FAIRLY COMMON,
DISCUSSIONS OF BANNING PLASTIC
ALTOGETHER ARE NOT.

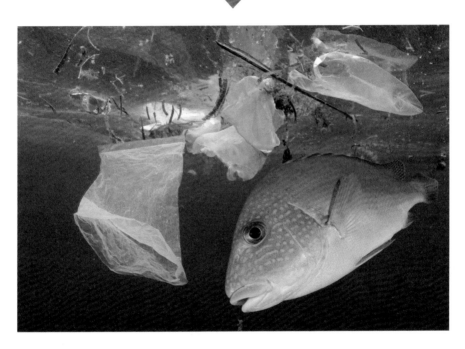

Ask yourself about the source of the information. Is it from a source you can trust? Does the story include complete information? Are the story's facts backed up by trustworthy sources? Is the writer trying to inform in an unbiased way? If the answer to any of these questions is no, it might be propaganda.

Looking at Bias

We should look for bias in any news we see or read. But we should also be aware of our own personal biases. A variety of media outlets present only the stories that back up opinions we already hold. This can make us less flexible in our thinking. It can cause us to overlook our own biases.

Can you figure out which stories you come across are real and which ones are fake?

You can't avoid propaganda. It's part of our culture. But if we know how to spot it, we can help break the cycle. We can focus on what is real and important and push the fake news aside.

One of these papers is the real *Washington Post*. The other is not. Which one do you think is the phony?

Real or Fake?

Is this story real or fake? See the Fake News Toolkit on page 29 to help you decide.

NEWS   [Search]   **Friday, February 22**

FRONT PAGE   **NEWS**   SPORTS   VARIETY   LIFESTYLE   COMICS   WANT ADS

EXPOSING GOVERNMENT!

Breaking news! Human beings have never walked on the moon. Documents not yet available to the public prove that the 1969 moon landing was a hoax. It was all staged on a film set. Even one of the astronauts on the mission admitted it. For his protection, his name is being withheld.

Fake! Some people believe this is true. But the story here gives you plenty of reasons to doubt it. The documents aren't available to the public, so they can't be checked. Plus, the astronaut is unnamed, and none of the story's sources can be checked. You can toss this one out as fake news without a second thought.

Scan the QR code to try another example.

Fake News Toolkit

When you watch or read a news story, it can be difficult to spot fake news. People want you to believe what they believe. Many try hard to convince you, even if they have to lie or twist facts. Read on to arm yourself with some tools for spotting fake news.

Consider the Source

Does the news come from a respected media source? News items that come from little-known sources are more likely to be fake. Learn about the organization that published the story. Is its purpose to provide fair, objective news?

Look for Objectivity

If an article tells only one side of a story, it might be fake news. A good news story should look at an issue from all sides and let readers come to their own conclusions.

Check the Facts

Don't just accept any information that a news story gives you. Follow up. Find out where the information comes from. Do the figures and surprising facts presented come with sources? And if they do, can you follow up on them?

Don't Spread It

If you see a story that you think might be fake news, don't spread it! Don't like it or share it. Don't even click on it. The best way to make fake news go away is to ignore it.

Report It

Google, Facebook, and many other websites now have buttons that allow you to report fake news. If you are sure an item is fake, report it. That can help stop the spread of the story and prevent it from fooling others.

Glossary

bias: the tendency to favor or oppose a particular group, idea, or person

Communism: a way of organizing a country's economy so that all the land, property, businesses, and resources belong to the government or community, and the profits are shared by all

context: all the things that affect something, such as the setting

hoax: a trick that makes people believe something that is not true

mainstream media: traditional forms of communication and news, such as network television, newspapers, and radio

objective: fair and based on verifiable facts instead of opinions or feelings

patriotism: love for one's country

skeptic: a person who often questions or doubts things such as claims or statements

social media: websites through which people create online communities to share information, ideas, personal messages, and more

viral: spreading very quickly to many people, especially through the internet

Learn More about Propaganda

Books

Harris, Duchess. *Uncovering Bias in the News*. Minneapolis: Core Library, 2018. This book looks at bias in the mainstream media and how it affects news coverage.

Jeffries, Joyce. *What's Fake News?* New York: KidHaven, 2019. What does the term *fake news* really mean? And how do politicians use the term for their own benefit? Read more about fake news, media bias, and misinformation.

Mara, Wil. *Mainstream News*. Ann Arbor, MI: Cherry Lake, 2018. Learn to ask questions about news coverage from mainstream media sources and develop the skills to spot fake news.

Websites

FactCheck.org
https://www.factcheck.org
FactCheck.org is one of the internet's leading websites for determining whether a news story is real or fake.

How Newspapers Work
https://people.howstuffworks.com/newspaper.htm
Learn more about the newspaper industry, including how editorial decisions on news stories are made.

How to Spot Fake News
https://kids.nationalgeographic.com/explore/ngk-sneak-peek/april-2017/fake-news/
Can you spot fake news? Check out this site for some tips and tricks.

Index

Photo Acknowledgments

Image credits: Chris Niedenthal/Getty Images, pp. 4, 5; Michael Nicholson/Getty Images, p. 6; Library of Congress (LC-DIG-ppmsca-50984), p. 7; DJ Dates/Alamy Stock Photo, p. 8; Jeff Morgan 07/Alamy Stock Photo, p. 9; Alex Wong/Getty Images, p. 10 (left); SOPA Images/Getty Images, pp. 10 (right), 26; Everett Historical/Shutterstock.com, p. 11; Library of Congress (LC-DIG ds 00989), p. 12; The New York Historical Society/Getty Images, p. 13; Photo 12/Getty Images, p. 14; Hulton Archive/Getty Images, p. 15; Courtesy of the National Library of Medicine, p. 16; Leigh Vogel/ Stringer/Getty Images, p. 17; NurPhoto/Getty Images, p. 18; Rawpixel.com/Shutterstock.com, p. 19; PjrStudio/Alamy Stock Photo, p. 20; AP Photos/ Jon Elswick, p. 21; bgblue/Getty Images, p. 22 (newspaper); Petar Tasevski/Shutterstock.com, p. 22 (plate); LightField Studios/Shutterstock.com, p. 23; Andriy Blokhin/Shutterstock.com, p. 24; Rich Carey/Shutterstock.com, p. 25; The Washington Post/Getty Images, p. 27; NASA/ JSC, p. 28 (both).

Cover: Library of Congress (LC-DIG-ppmsc-03521).

Learn More about Propaganda

Books

Harris, Duchess. *Uncovering Bias in the News.* Minneapolis: Core Library, 2018. This book looks at bias in the mainstream media and how it affects news coverage.

Jeffries, Joyce. *What's Fake News?* New York: KidHaven, 2019. What does the term *fake news* really mean? And how do politicians use the term for their own benefit? Read more about fake news, media bias, and misinformation.

Mara, Wil. *Mainstream News.* Ann Arbor, MI: Cherry Lake, 2018. Learn to ask questions about news coverage from mainstream media sources and develop the skills to spot fake news.

Websites

FactCheck.org
https://www.factcheck.org
FactCheck.org is one of the internet's leading websites for determining whether a news story is real or fake.

How Newspapers Work
https://people.howstuffworks.com/newspaper.htm
Learn more about the newspaper industry, including how editorial decisions on news stories are made.

How to Spot Fake News
https://kids.nationalgeographic.com/explore/ngk-sneak-peek/april-2017/fake-news/
Can you spot fake news? Check out this site for some tips and tricks.

Index

Photo Acknowledgments

Image credits: Chris Niedenthal/Getty Images, pp. 4, 5; Michael Nicholson/Getty Images, p. 6; Library of Congress (LC-DIG-ppmsca-50984), p. 7; DJ Dates/Alamy Stock Photo, p. 8; Jeff Morgan 07/Alamy Stock Photo, p. 9; Alex Wong/Getty Images, p. 10 (left); SOPA Images/Getty Images, pp. 10 (right), 26; Everett Historical/Shutterstock.com, p. 11; Library of Congress (LC-DIG-ds-00989), p. 12; The New York Historical Society/Getty Images, p. 13; Photo 12/Getty Images, p. 14; Hulton Archive/Getty Images, p. 15; Courtesy of the National Library of Medicine, p. 16; Leigh Vogel/ Stringer/Getty Images, p. 17; NurPhoto/Getty Images, p. 18; Rawpixel.com/Shutterstock.com, p. 19; PjrStudio/Alamy Stock Photo, p. 20; AP Photos/ Jon Elswick, p. 21; bgblue/Getty Images, p. 22 (newspaper); Petar Tasevski/Shutterstock.com, p. 22 (plate); LightField Studios/Shutterstock.com, p. 23; Andriy Blokhin/Shutterstock.com, p. 24; Rich Carey/Shutterstock.com, p. 25; The Washington Post/Getty Images, p. 27; NASA/ JSC, p. 28 (both).

Cover: Library of Congress (LC-DIG-ppmsc-03521).